INVERSELY CONVERSE - 6

A SPACE PHILOSOPHY

WILLIAM OMPRAKASH

No.8, 3rd Cross Street,CIT Colony,
Mylapore, Chennai, Tamil Nadu-600004

ISBN 978-1-63606-266-2

I DEDICATE THIS BOOK TO MY PARENTS AND FRIENDS.

Contents

CHAPTER ONE

LAWS OF INVERSELY CONVERSE

Law 1: Extension of old one

Law 2a: Inability to choose a tool though the object is fit enough for the thesis.

Law 2b: Follow your thoughts not mind reading.

Law 3 (a): Work against work

Law 3(b) work inside work

Law 4: Dirty Subject and eternal discovery get coagulated to new prototype which mattered mostly and hence the disappearance of the respective subject..

Law 5: man made objects are none in the space, all are change of form to another Or a new Reason can be stated irrespecctive of ettc.,.

Law 6: Nothing is essential , all matter and their properties are intertwined and so it is never ending ....

Law 7: Birth of space ...or their is nothing called aging GOD

Law 8: sensible philosophy cant be identified, only realiized

Law 9: materialistic world exercised well enough leads to new progressive environment .

Law 10: Divine intervention and the urge to find the new object leads to victory.

Law 11:Life of the to be victorious subject and hence the new miracle.

Law 12:"Fiction or Fact " both are interchangeable.

Law 13: New concept cant impact the respective society immediately.

Law 14:More the debate ; more will be the resilence and everlasting of the invention or discovery.

Law 15: Petulant or to become annoyed remarks are essential , which we call as critics.

Law 16. Origin of thoughts for any invention could be some cause.

Law 17: Application of any new theory normally not predetermined in most of the cases.

Law 18. Exhaust or exclaimed after invention should exist .

Law 19: "Jack of all or Master of all ", meaning attempting to develop metaskill leads to knowledge hunger
.

Law 20:Welfare to the society and hence every new creation has some creation as origin.

Law 21: Beginning and Ending of inversely converse exists only if source of space is an identified one.

Law 22: Nature of inversely converse remains dirty and entangled one ,but the ecstasy which we draw out of it is immense pleasure .

Law 23: Laws so far and to come in future are all from one source which is law 2(b) which is " follow your thoughts not mind reading.

Law 24: Reinvent law2(b) very often.

Law 25:Is nothing but law 1... meaning "inversely converse means extension of the old thing or phrase or invention etc...meaning all law are spiral in nature.

CHAPTER TWO

Laws of Inversely Converse in calculus

Law 1: new derivations are coming up which are extensions to the old one...

Law 2:when new concept arises and if no other tool to support the concept

Law 3a:for any invention or miracles or peace process or wars or ceremonies or political debates to become successful following the respective individual thoughts are necessary.

Law 3b: Work inside work

Inside L - Hospital rule if many equations comes up then it is work inside work.

Law 3a :Work against work

L - Hospital rule and chain rule are Inversely Converse.

Law 4: Newton was a dirty man and calculus is eternal entity because of which till now got so many new prototypes developed by Einstein and physicts as well.

Law 5: as of now, little philosophical one. Sometimes invention happened because of divine intervention which comes under law 10 as well.

Law 6: calculus and their properties like for e.g. limits are intertwined.

Law 7: Big explanation needed. Tell u later.

Law 12: when calculus gave birth it was fiction after which it becomes fact.

Law 13: new concept can't be tàken by the society immediately which everyone knows .

Law 14: calculus took long Time to establish.As for any theory application is must. Sometimes it need not be required.

Law 18: once calculus invented and was accepted by contemporary mathematicians , the inventor was excited and exhausted.

Law 15: Before establishment of calculus lot of criticisms was encountered by the inventor.

Law 16: why calculus was invented?to establish a concept calculus was invented.

Law 17: Calculus was invented in 16th century. It has still has wider applications which was not foreseen.

Law 14: Before calculus established it underwent lot of debates between mathematicians like who , how ..or was it a piracy etc.,.

Law 13: calculus didn't create huge impact in the society during its initial days.

Law 23: followed till now .. example is Laplace, Fourier, and many more to come....

Law 24 and law 25 will be explained later..

CHAPTER THREE

Botany and Mathematics are inversely Converse.....

In mathematics all obeys all laws of inversely Converse .In trigonometry sin theta and Cosec theta are inversely Converse .Again cosine theta and secant theta are inversely Converse. Similarly tan theta and Cot theta are inversely Converse .

Angle of elevation and angle of depression are inversely Converse.

work against work in Algebra and work inside work in trigonometry .not only in Algebra, trignometry but also in permutation and combination .

work against work itself is an Inversely Converse to work inside .

ordinary differential equations is an inversely Converse to partial differential equation. again law 3a and 3b of work inside work and work against Work are satisfied.

inference :

As of mathematics and as of now ,mathematics obeys all laws of inversely Converse.

Phase 2 of Law of inversely Converse:

you plant something and you can uproot something. yes it is an inversely Converse. but how, whatever we planted has grown. still it obeys inversely Converse.

For example 1: In botany we sow seeds plants are grown Law1 is satisfied similarly law3a and law 3b satisfied

For example 2:in mathematics new concept comes after a while inverse of the concept by default happened weather by divine intervention or because of some necessities.

Fiction or Fact:

Initially all the proposals are fiction once established it becomes fact. After undefined quantum of time fact becomes extinct . In other words extinct itself becomes another fiction may or may not be similar to the old ones from where it was born.

CHAPTER FOUR

De addiction and inversely Converse

Definition of addiction :

Anything which becomes unmanageable is addiction. not necessarily drug addiction it could be knowledge addiction, food addiction, tour addiction, beverages addiction and so on. is it wrong in getting along with addiction forever .it is not exactly wrong .Based upon how it affects society or our own well being it is measured. for example if one wants to pursue education rather I would say knowledge he or she has to learn and over a period of time get addicted to it .it is because of such addiction any miracle or rather I would say any invention happened for example Marie Curie inventions used to kill cancer . During the process of invention the harmful rays killed her gradually. But that addiction is a positive one simply because the invented entity is a boon to the medical community. similarly like what Edison did .similarly great personalities are hard core addicts in pursuing the knowledge. now tell me whether it is good or bad.

co founder of Microsoft Corporation Bill Gates still after

money though he is a philanthropist. yes too much of money is also addiction .

coming to saint too much of thought about god is also addiction .another typical example is Ramanujan, a greatest Indian mathematician was a hard core addict in coming up with new ideas and theorems or formulas in mathematics. he passed away at the age of 32.

how to come out of it ? Is it possible .

possible by repeated practice .if one denied of something and after he achieved that he suddenly felt that his potential exploded and he want to pursue. so how he or she can stop this Unstoppable pursue of addiction. my theological reply is fate. All are predetermined.

like what happened to Newton, Einstein, GD Naidu, Ramanujan, Faraday , Henry Ford and so on.

at one point of time one has to think not only about his own well being but also about the society there by he or she will reduce the addicted habit .
the process of reducing itself is an deaddiction .

To how long or she has to reduce it .This time philosophical one simply because one has achieved to certain extent and so live for others . Which is what the Motto .' live for others ' Moto doesn't mean selfless living. keep your physical and mental strength strong.
Things will fall in place .

conclusionon :

constant pursuing what looks initially as an alien habit and later on loved too much . During the process unable to come out of it is an addiction. when realised deaddiction begins. so after addiction, deaddiction surfaces .now law 1 of inversaly converse satisfied .

similarly you can practice deaddiction against addiction which is work against work . it is also work inside work.

law 2a :"inability to choose a tool though the object is fit enough for the thesis.
meaning no proper medication to come out of any addiction completely .

Meaningng there is no tangible tool though deaddiction is fit enough for thesis. Sheer will Power will motivate one to come out of addiction . Though pills support you.

Law 2b: "Followyour thoughts not mind reading ".
meaning when ever thought of going after drugs or alcohol or Knowledge pursuing draw a Prototype to come out of it . mostly ,as of addicts those thoughts are common. Based on situations or scenarios it might very.

CHAPTER FIVE

Ten steps to become like Einstein

Ten steps to become like Einstein

step 1 Do Paperwork consistently.

step 2 Try to use brain alone . no outside physical entities to understand
a concept

step 3 Learn the making of Legends.

step 4 Learn the concept and try to draw out various probable behind the scenes of it.

step 5 Learn, assimilate, learn assimilate and learn continuously throughout your life .

step 6 As we gain skill and knowledge try to follow above 5 steps repeatedly which gives a new skill known as metaskill.

step 7 Now the most important one. which is discard pen and paper and solve any given problem in mind itself it is called or known as thought experiments.

step 8 Now the next highest step is close both your palm and keep your mouth closed and arrive a solution for a given problem through thoughts alone .

step 9 Do step 8 for years or months which I leave it to individuals discretion.

Step 10 while doing above 9 steps see to that you maintain your balance.

CHAPTER SIX

Stress Management and Inversely converse

Stress management

Why we are going for a stress or why we are undergoing stress. Millenniums back life was not that much complicated. Now then fittest of the survival plays pivotal role in every ones walk of life. Right from family management, to finance management to human management to spiritual management and so on.

In every day walks of life ,looking at the present situation life becomes highly competitive one . Stress is a nomenclature , Rather I would say few days back stress remains jargon for common man. But now, many job competition , examination which validate one's competency, career growth,

health hazards and so many other things are there. Money management is not easier as it involves job, family, children education, medical check up. Other auxillary expenses are pilgrimage visits, abroad tours , diplomatic tours, mercantile purposes or trade visits etc.,.

How to manage stress using inversely converse.

Before getting into it, I will briefly narrate the purpose of inversely converse. Inversely converse not necessarily a philosophical jargon. It is in daily walks of life. My suggestion to manage stress is inversely converse.

Now then inversely converse in psychology . "psycho" means "mind" . "logy" means "study of". Inversely converse has 25 laws. If one applies not necessary 25 laws still he or she can recover from stress. All laws of inversely converse can be applied in psychology as well.

Law 1. Extension of old one. This law can be very easily applied in psychology .

New developments are coming up in psychology. The subject or person which gets affected by stress can sought the guidance of psychologists.

How extension of old one?

Subject underwent a problem and psychologists suggesting a solution is a new one.

Meaning the problem is old one .Extension of old one is solution.

Law 2a: Inability to chose a tool though the object is fit enough for the thesis.

Psychologists has no concrete tool for the object's problem though the object is fit enough for the thesis. Meaning here object refers to a person . The problem is for any stress issues there is no concrete tool. The probable tools which is in the industry are motivational speech , identifying one's problem through counselling sessions and so on. Here the thesis refers to the person or subject or object who have undergone some kind of stress.

Law 2b : Follow your thoughts not mind reading

For stress best solution is the respective individual has to think or give a thought about stress or Rather I would say the origin of it " follow his or her thoughts after which he or she can identify the core problem and come out of it instead of mind reading. Here one raises the query why mind reading , because mind reading will complicate the issues. Sometimes people call follow your thoughts close to introspection which is not so . understanding law 2b i.e follow your thoughts not mind reading requires more practice.

Law 3a: work against work.

Distress or Eustress are one typical example for law 3 a . likewise ,

law 3b work inside work.

Under stress , "distress and eustress "are classified which is work inside work.

Law 12 fiction or fact both are interchangeable.

Identifying the term stress wouldn't have been recognized so it was fiction. Later on it become fact as it was used to identify the state of mind of any individual.

Law 13: new concept cant impact the respective society immediately.

The word stress was not unknown to too many people . According to law 12 , if we extrapolate law 12 , law 13 comes into picture.

Law 10 divine intervention and the urge to find the new object leads to victory

law 10 cant be justified based on law 2b as well . Meaning divine intervention plays a role though medication also exists.

Law 11 life of the victorious subject and hence the new miracle

Though stress , it just played a role in once life and there is every chance that the respective individual become victorious which is a new miracle

law 8 sensible philosophy cant be identified one realized.

CHAPTER SEVEN

Differential equation(For Family of curves) and inversely converse:

Law 1. Differential equation is an extension of calculus.

Law 2a. Inability to choose a tool thought the object is fit enough for the thesis .

For all scientific applications there was hardly a tool before differential equations.

Law 2b. Follow your thoughts not mind reading.

"Necessity to find a solution which crept in the mind is follow your thoughts."

Law 3a Work against work.

Differential equations depends on polynomial and analytical geometry ,which is work against work.

Law 3b Work inside work.

Differential equations is a subset of calculus and hence work inside work.

Law 4 :Dirty subject and eternal discovery get coagulated to new prototype which mattered mostly and hence the disappearance of the respective subject.

Differential equation invented and innovated by many legends which i presume to be dirty subject. Differential equation is an eternal discovery of scientific application are concerned. It is a common fact that invented entity remain eternal and remembered for years as its impact in scientific community is huge , whereas the inventor or then subject which invented differential equation was not remembered for years.

Law 5 Man made objects are none in the space all are change of form or another or a new reason can be stated irrespective of etc.,.

Differential equation is an invented entity which are made out of other stand alone tools like analytical geometry, trignometry which again is made of numbers which again made out of vertical columns asb because during ancient days number system was not born. Therefore differential equation as a man objects which are derived from stand alone tools like trigonometry etc.,.. and hence law 5 satisfied.

Law 6 Nothing is essential all matter and there properties are intertwined and so it is never ending.

Differential equation is a matter and slope of family of curves is a property.

Law 7 Birth of space or there is nothing called aging god.

Having seen so many other application of inversely converse till now let us now dig into law 7 applied here in differential equation,... because here birth of space relates to differential equation. Not only anything "over, below and above" sky is space like trees , plants, animals trigonometry , batter, wine ,calculus are all part of space , hence birth of space, since no one knows birth of space rather I would say there is not thing called aging god which means birth of differential calculus (space) not known and hence god which no I presume as god is not ageing simply because the invented entity wont die therefore not ageing.

Law 8: Sensible philosophy can't be identified.

True , at times some philosophies cant be identified only realized for example differential equation is a sensible philosophy because before invention it was not identified only realized which we can corroborate by referring the history of the respective philosophy.

law 9 Materialistic world exercised well enough leads to new progressive environment.

Differential equation exercised by scientific community which also comes under materialistic world leads to new progressive environment meaning new giant leaps in science.

Law 10 Divine intervention and the urge to find the new object leads to victory.

For any new invention ,divine intervention was or is must and hence urge to find the new object or entity.

Law 12 Fiction or Fact both are interchangeable.

Differential equation initially was fiction later on based on it application it becomes fact which all critic accepts unanimously.

Law 13: New concept cant impact the respective society immediately

Very true. Right from calculus meaning differential calculus to the currently on going discussion differential equation who impact the respective society immediately.

Law 14: More the debate more will be the resilience and everlasting of the invention or discovery

Any concept or theory to be proved and accepted lot of debate has to be undergo which is healthier then only resilience and everlasting of the invention or discovery exists.

Law 15 Petulant or to become annoyed remarks are essential, which we call as criticswhich is an extension of law 14. Meaning annoyed remarks are essential which everyone of us call as critics.

Law 16 Origin of thoughts for any invention could be some cause.

Law 16 has little discrepancy simply because not all thoughts some cause but some has for differential equation whose origin of thoughts is a need of a tool for scientific application like analysing the behaviour of space bodies.

Law17. Application if any new theory normally not predetermined in most of the cases.

Very true some new concept surface in the mind of an inventor without even knowing its application. Later on some subject felt the usage of it.

Law 18. Exhaust of exclaimed after invention should exist.

After any subject which come up with new entity or invention exhaust or exclaimed would have happened.

Law 19. "Jack or all trades or master of all trades "meaning attempting to develop metaskill leads to knowledge hunger.

As of this law 19 for differential equation can be dealt later.

Law 20: Welfare to the society and hence every new creation has some creation of origin.

well said, as of differential equation, differential and integral calculus was the origin.

Law 21: Beginning and ending of inversely converse exists only if source of space is an identified one.

Again very true, advent of differential equation not known though empirically some date given which leads to source of space is an unidentified one.

Law 22 Nature of inversely converse remains dirty and entangled one, but the ecstasy which we draw out of its is immense pleasure.

Again very very true, it needs big explanation we can discuss it later.

Law 23 and law 24 and law 256 will be explained later.

CHAPTER EIGHT

Inversely converse in poetry

Law 1 :Extension of old one

Meaning new dimension in poetry comes either after knowledge from the primitive or ancient one which is an extension of old one.

Law 2b: Follow your thoughts not mind reading

Poetic skill takes a giant leap when we follow thoughts instead of mind reading.

Law 2a: Inability to choose a tool though the object is fit enough for the thesis.

There is no crystal clear tool to write a poetry which is the thesis or object to be implemented in writing. The tool here refer to the knowledge and skill which we acquired together with the imagination.

Law 3a : Work against work

Poetry written by **William Shakespeare**and poetry also by **William Wordsworth**. It is very evident that wordsworth works came into existence after Shakespeare which is " work against work"

Law 3b: Work inside work

Works created by Shakespeare alone satisfies work inside work. Following statement is not a paradox. "

Shakespeare invented 1700 new words". Those vocabulary was implemented or adopted by other poets who came after him. Meaning new words are new works. Hence the re-usage of those words in a different poems by different poet is a work against work. Again if the invented vocabulary by Shakespeare used in a different poem by Shakespeare. Meaning it is " work inside work".

Law 4: Dirty subject and eternal discovery get coagulated to new prototype which mattered mostly and hence the disappearance of the respective subject.

Shakespeare is a dirty subject and his poetry work is a new prototype which mattered mostly and hence the disappearance of the respective subject. Here the subject is Shakespeare .

Law 5: Man made objects are none in the space. All are change of form to another or a new reason can be stated irrespective of etc.,.

Again very true. Not even a grain of sand can be created from nowhere. Therefore man made objects are none in the space. It is just out of probabilities or possibilities new objects are converted. Rather I would say transformed.

Law 6: Nothing is essential, all matter and their properties are intertwined and so it is never ending.

Sonnet is a matter, each and every line in a sonnet are properties. Sonnet defined as fourteen lines. Sonnet and each and every line are intertwined.

Law 7: Birth of space or there is nothing called ageing god.

i).Here space refers to a poem .ii). other words poem is also part of space. Going by i). space is made out of poems meaning all are confined in a poem . meaning poem alone exists in space. In other words space may be treated as a misnomer and so can be replaced as " poem". Going by ii).space includes earth, sun, galaxy, comets, trees, fruits, meaning poems, novels incandescent lamb or bulb , petrol are also part of space.

So coming to law 7 ,space or poem or calculus or heart or brain , president of America are all can be born .Now the hypotheses which I am going to take is they all belongs to space and so , of which are transformed or decayed . My conclusion over here is " birth of space " is an unidentified one as per inversely converse or in other words there is nothing called ageing god. Here god is poem. Poem comes in B.C. or A.D. and to come in future might get old which may not be applicable.

Law 8: Sensible philosophy cant be identified only realized.

Any philosophy are realized after futile or fruitful attempts. Al the philosophies , in other words all those we come across are philosophies. Which we may perceive or not depends upon one's involvement. Some philosophies like those which falls under inversely converse ,at least one law are sensible philosophies.

Law 9: Materialistic world exercised well enough leads to new progressive environment.

Based upon individual's perspective or experience which they acquired over period of time one classify or state that experience as materialistic or spiritualistic world. What looks materialistic may apear as spiritualistic to some ultimately it leads to new progressive environment. Here any poem speaks about or so called the thought gives a new progressive environment meaning new evolution or revolution happen.

Law 10: Divine intervention and the urge to find the new object leads to victory.

At times we feel or realized divine intervention either accidentally or incidentally would have happened or occurred which leads to new art or creativity in other words poetry which is applicable here which we can call as victory.

Law 11: Life of the to be victorious subject and hence the new miracle.

Here the victorious subject refers to the creator or inventor. The noun " creator" comes when a " verb" poem penned.

Law 12: " Fiction or fact " both are interchangeable.

To start with ,initially ,in most of the cases poem referred as fiction. Later over a period of time we might feel it becomes part of life . similarly we can take or treat that " fact" meaning both are interchangeable.

Law 13: New concept cant impact the respective society immediately.

"poem which we treat here as a new concept and hence cant impact the respective society immediately. Yes over a period of time it creates a impact in the society.

Law 14: more the debate more will be the resilience and everlasting of the invention or discovery,.

Any art or creation has to undergo the debate. Only then corresponding invention or discovery creates everlasting or resilience will happen.

Law 15: Petulant or annoyed remarks are essential , which we call as critics.

Again , I keep saying annoyed remarks are always essential , then only the poem will stand firm over millennium after millennium .

Law 16: Origin of thoughts for any invention could be some cause.

Any poem needs inspiration . either from inside or outside of human anatomy. Meaning without inspiration not even a single entity either tangible or intangible occur.

Law 17: Application of any new theory normally not predetermined in most of the cases.

Poem to start with may not have proper application. Over a period of time its usages are determined. Having said above, without even aware of the application some poem would have transformed.

Law 18: Exhaust or exclaimed after invention should exist.

Any invention or creativity after it is done, exhaust or exclaimed should occur. After poem penned out ,any poet has to undergo exclaimed or exhaustion.

Rest of the laws we can discuss later.